KW-458-965

"Hurry along children!" says Miss Fuss, "the bus is waiting." But Theo is not very happy about leaving his ring behind.

THEO

learns to swim

3701144868
358
i/c

FRANCIS CLOSE HALL
LEARNING CENTRE
Road
Cheltenham
Tel (01

Theo can't wait to go to school this morning. His class is going swimming for the first time today. "Can I take my new rubber ring?" he asks Daddy, as he gets out of bed.

The Sports Centre looks very big and grand from the outside. "I bet it's got a huge swimming pool!" says Lulu excitedly.

"Look! That's clever!" says Theo, pointing to a girl who is doing a hand-stand on the mat. "I'm going to try that when I get home."

Both Miss Fuss and Miss Pott have to help some of the children to get changed. Lulu's ready first, but Theo has only just found his blue and white swimming trunks.

"I wish we had a big strong shower like this at home,"
thinks Theo. "It's like standing in the rain, but it's
lovely and warm."

"Move your arms and kick your legs," says Mr. Pike, the swimming instructor. "That's the way to stay afloat in the water."

"You must never run around a swimming pool," he tells the children. "Now show me how well you can walk around it."

"Don't worry, Theo, I will hold you. Just stretch out your arms and relax."

Everybody in Theo's class is concentrating very hard. They have to swim from the edge to the steps. It's fun, but exhausting.

"The best way to go forward is to keep kicking," calls Mr. Pike.

"Careful!" calls Miss Pott, but its too late. Theo was so busy watching the divers, that he didn't see the edge of the pool. Now he's dived in himself!

"But look! I can swim all by myself! This is good!" thinks Theo. Amy says, "You can give your rubber ring to Paul now," as she helps him out of the pool.

THEO DISCOVERS THE WORLD

Dear Parents,

These delightful stories, with their charming illustrations, are intended for you to enjoy with your child.

Set aside a quiet time to share the book and give yourselves the pleasure of each other's company. Use the illustrations as a stimulus for conversation, as a starting point for your imagination. Allow your child to discover the satisfaction of reading as communication.

The text is deliberately kept short, but acts as a springboard for discussion between you. With the very young this may go no further than looking at the lively illustrations and identifying objects, colours and situations. With older children it may also include concepts of their own relationships, emotions, behaviour. Respond to any comments, answer any questions and talk about what is or might be happening in each picture.

Theo lives in Spain and children are children all over the world. Take this opportunity to explore differences and similarities between people and cultures at home and abroad. The guidelines below are a few suggestions of topics that might come up for discusssion on each page.

Let the child take you by the hand and lead you through the book.

Jana Pattenden

Waking up. What is Mummy packing in the bag? What is Daddy doing to help this morning? Why does Baby Paul look so unhappy? What will Theo have to do to get ready for school? What else will Mummy have to do? What will Daddy do? What do you think Baby Paul will do while Theo is at school? Talk about swimming. Have you ever been? Where do you go? Can you swim? Do you like it? What's the use of a rubber ring?

The sports centre. What activities can you do in a Sports Centre? Why are there so many windows? Why is the building so big and tall? Why are there two buildings? Is the Sports Centre in the centre of town? What is the man on the ladder doing? Why is the bicycle under the tree? How many of the houses have got T.V.s? Talk about using a pedestrian crossing.

The gym. Have you ever been to a gym club? What clothes should you wear to do gym? What gym apparatus can you see in the picture? What can you do on each piece of equipment? Why do some of the children have to wait? Can you do the splits? Can you do handstands? Help your child to do somersaults.

Off we go! What are all the children wearing? Why? What do you think they have got in their bags? Why does Theo leave his rubber ring behind? Who is going to look after it? Why is he unhappy about it? Why are the children getting into a bus? What are other people in the picture doing?

The changing room. Why is it important to keep everying in your bag when you have changed? What is the boy looking at through the window? Why does Miss Fuss have to help Edward? Why do some children prefer to change in the cubicle? Talk about getting dressed and undressed — buttons, buckles, zips and laces.